Feeding the Wild Rabbit

Feeding the Wild Rabbit

Poems by

Angela Patten

© 2024 Angela Patten. All rights reserved.
This material may not be reproduced in any form, published,
reprinted, recorded, performed, broadcast,
rewritten, or redistributed without
the explicit permission of Angela Patten.
All such actions are strictly prohibited by law.

Cover design by Shay Culligan
Cover art by Zak Patten
"By Cutler Pond at Sunset"
Author photo by Daniel Lusk

ISBN: 978-1-63980-662-1
Library of Congress Control Number: 2024950127

Kelsay Books
502 South 1040 East, A-119
American Fork, Utah 84003
Kelsaybooks.com

For Daniel

Acknowledgments

Poems in this collection first appeared in the following journals and anthologies:

Calyx Journal: "Last Time I Saw My Sisters"
Cloudbank 16: "The Hidden Life of Words"
Epiphany: "This"
Even The Daybreak: 35 Years of Salmon Poetry (Ireland): "The Writing Process"
Innisfree Poetry Review: "Out in Left Field at Dodgertown, Florida," "Sweet Aftons"
Live Encounters: "Feeding the Wild Rabbit," "Geese—a Love Poem," "Green Up Day at the Superfund Site," "Hard Evidence," "Lingering over It," "Linguistic Anthropology," "Making Strange," "Mono Lake," "Motherhood," "Signs of Bad Weather," "Springtime at Starbucks," "The Bird of Praise," "The Pancake Artist," "The Place Where Poetry Happens," "The Sinking of the Isolda," "The Window," "Wellfleet"
The Main Street Rag: "This Is the Life"
PoemCity (Montpelier, VT): "Persistence Hunting," "Things I Never Say Aloud," "On the La Platte"
PoemCity Anthology 2024: "On the La Platte"
Poetry India: "Swinging Boats"
The Raven's Perch: "Blood Moon," "Of Saints & Secrets," "Past Life Regression Moryah," "The Weight of the World"
Saint Katherine Review: "Inchigeelagh Getaway," "Why I Would Like to Be a River"
Sylvia Magazine (UK): "Idle Hands"
Tiny Moments Literary Magazine, Vol III: "Any Questions"
The Wexford Bohemian (Ireland): "Shine" [1]

---

[1] Winner of the 2022 Anthony Cronin International Short Poem Award

Poetry Collections by Angela Patten

Feeding the Wild Rabbit

The Oriole & the Ovenbird

In Praise of Usefulness

Reliquaries

Still Listening

Contents

The Hidden Life of Words	13
The Writing Process	17
Linguistic Anthropology	18
The Place Where Poetry Happens	20
Swallowing the Lexicon	21
This	23
Syntax	25
Any Questions?	26
The Bird of Praise	27
A Call to Prayer	28
Springtime at Starbucks	29
The Pancake Artist	31
Polishing the Floor	32
The Window	34
The Sinking of the *Isolda*	35
Idle Hands	37
Of Saints and Secrets	39
My Parents Were Always Kneeling	41
In Ísle Brí (in low spirits, Irish)	42
Signs of Bad Weather	44
Tissue Paper	45
Sweet Aftons	47
Shine	48
The Joyful Mysteries	49
Speaking of Things That Are No Longer in Use	50
Making Strange	52
Black Babies	53
Cures for Insomnia	55
Swinging Boats	57
A Fine Romance	59
In the Adirondacks There Is a Town Called Paradox	60
Past Life Regression Moryah	62

Out in Left Field at Dodgertown, Florida	64
Last Time I Saw My Sisters	65
Things I Never Say Aloud	66
Motherhood	67
Feeding the Wild Rabbit	68
Inchigeelagh Getaway	70
The Suspension of Disbelief	72
Blood Moon	73
Green Up Day at the Superfund Site	74
Domestic Science	75
Soundscape of My Ear	77
Lingering Over It	78
Persistence Hunting	79
Umwelt	80
Geese—A Love Poem	81
Wellfleet	83
Mono Lake, California	84
The Weight of the World	85
On the La Platte	86
This Is the Life	87
Why I Would Like to Be a River	88

The Hidden Life of Words

1.
Clavichord: a musical instrument that produces
pleasing sounds when brass or iron strings
are struck with metal blades called *tangents*.
From the Latin *clavis* "key" and *chordis* "string."

2.
Clavicle: the slender S-shaped bone
that serves as a strut between shoulderblade
and breastbone. The only long bone
in the body that lies horizontally.

Its Latin name *clavicula* means "little key,"
perhaps because the human voice arises
from that indentation in the throat where
the left clavicle curves to meet the right.

The wishbone, *furcula,* means "little fork."
Found in birds and sometimes dinosaurs,
it is formed by the fusion of two clavicles.

The town of Belle Fourche ("Beautiful Fork")
was named by French explorers when they beheld
the confluence of two South Dakota rivers.

In the choice between two equal forks,
which one to choose for *Amuse Bouche*
and which for *Croque Monsieur?*

3.
Tangent: as in a straight line or plane,
touching but not intersecting, a curve
or curved surface. Also a completely
different line of thought or action.

According to the media, the collarbone
is one of the most desirable bodily features
since women began flaunting theirs in public.

Think Audrey Hepburn as Holly Golightly,
her slender cigarette holder accentuating
the saltcellars sandwiched between
her collarbones in "Breakfast at Tiffany's."

Twenty minutes of shoulder-shrugs or yoga asanas
each day and you too can have prominent collarbones.
However, malnutrition will produce the same effect.

4.
Serpentine: the supple shape of a stream
murmuring by the roadside, going somewhere
I have never been.

Which brings me to the serpent, writhing
at the foot of the statue of Michael the Archangel,
placed at my child's eye level
as I raced across the immense vestibule
of Saint Michael's hospital, Dun Laoghaire.

5.
Sin: The nuns gave holy pictures as rewards
for being good, which meant not talking.
Was talking therefore a sin?

In elocution class I studied dipthongs, diaphragm,
larynx, lips and labials in order to ensure
that I would not be confused with someone
like myself, a child of the working poor.

The Midwest Society for Acoustic Ecology
celebrates World Listening Day each year
by asking us to pay attention
to our sonic surroundings—

a vernal pond loud with the sounds
of clamoring amphibians
newly resurrected from the mud,
each one proclaiming I am! I am!

6.
Venial: a sin that is slight and pardonable,
committed without full knowledge or full consent.
How one sin clasps the hand of another
as they slide down the sensual slope of pleasure.

How one syllable leapfrogs over the next,
gathering momentum, constructing associations,
opening linguistic windows to learn new words.

7.
Scold: a woman who nags or grumbles constantly.
Also shrew, fishwife, termagant, trollop.

Scold's Bridle: a medieval torture implement
used as a muzzle to publicly humiliate
"loquacious nagging or troublesome ladies"
and female prisoners. No doubt tears.
Metal and salt. Then silence.[1]

---

[1] Scold's Bridle: National Museum of Ireland—Archaeology, Kildare Street, Dublin

The Writing Process

Mornings I lie in bed sipping coffee
letting my mind off its weekday leash
to go roaming like a multicolored mongrel
following its moist nose, snuffling
under lichen, mud-loam
the leaf-mulch of the past.

Sometimes there's nothing much to show
for all my rooting at the tuberous rhizome
of family relationships, worrying
the labyrinthine radicle of memory.

Sometimes a few small bones
to chew over later by the fireplace—
crosspatch, snoutfair, colossive.
An archaic adage—*to be moithered
flummoxed, chuffed* by a chance remark
gnawed down to the marrow—
*her skin like bellows leather—
she was put to the pin of her collar—
he was forced to eat his words—*

Sometimes my ears twitch
head lifts as if at a tug
of the choke-chain, remembering
the moment each gobstopper
was winched up into the light.

Linguistic Anthropology

> "It's only words and words are all I have/to take your heart away."
> —The Bee Gees, "Words"

The story goes that once upon a time
the family of languages set off
on pilgrimage around the world.

Some traveled the trade routes of the East,
some took the waters in ancient springs.
All stayed connected like hands
clasping each other in a human chain.

Pidgin was spoken, goods were traded.
It was a glorious cacophony.

There are 7,097 living languages in the world today
though some are experiencing the aches of old age—
exhausted verbs, arthritic nouns—
and the difficulties of keeping up with the young.

In the New York Metro area
there are native speakers of 800 languages.
Imagine the verbal traffic-jams,
the nods and shrugs, the glottal stops,
the clicks and fricatives,
all that joyful noise.

But worldwide one language
dies out every fortnight.
Even the word 'fortnight' is threatened
with becoming merely 'two weeks'
any day now.

My father, the hardest-working man I've ever known,
was made redundant after 25 years on the job.
Think of that word—*redundant.*
How was a man to feel?

Sometimes forgotten words surface in my head
like bubbles rising in a stream—
plimsolls, jotter, hoover, father—
words I never questioned,
only took for the thing itself.

People keep inventing things,
then inventing names for them.
When will it stop?

When the last known speaker of a language dies,
it is called "language death."
Do the other languages lament,
each in its own tongue?

Cristina Calderón, last known native speaker
of the Yaghan language, died at 93.
I wonder what was the last thing she said?
And to whom?

The Place Where Poetry Happens

Sometimes it is an aviary echoing bird calls
or a concert-hall with a Steinway Grand,
a jazz club in the city with a tiny stage,
an upright bass, candles crammed
in Chianti bottles on the tables, couples
holding hands, half-listening to the music.

Sometimes I am invited in to listen
to a line or two, perhaps a wisp of dream
or glint of something shiny that swam up
from the depths into the net of memory,
turned and flicked its tail, swam out again,

but left an image that will unfurl
like a water lily, or a series of words
primed to explode on contact with the ear.

Swallowing the Lexicon

"I ate advertisements like sea waves eating a coastline"
—Major Jackson, from "The Language of the Moon"

The bright yellow package of *Kellogg's Rice Crispies*
sat on the table every morning and I ate
the copy word for word along with the milk
and the snap-crackle-pop. Likewise the spiel
on the *Cornflakes* box and also the *Puffed Rice*
package when we briefly deviated into that
culinary cul-de-sac in response to a radio ad.

On the double-decker bus my eye was transfixed
by the words *If you enjoy reading this, let
thousands of others read your advertisement!*
Then inexorably drawn to
Bovril—stops that sinking feeling! and
*Andrews Liver Salts—experience inner cleanliness
and enjoy life to the full.*

Depressed? a smiling face inquired.
A cup of good tea cheers you up!
(issued by the Tea Council of Ireland).

*National Brand Crimp Nylon Underwear
for Women and Teenagers, made from
BRI-LON with BANLON texture.*
The prospect did nothing to endear me
to my female fate. But all those lovely
cigarette ads, those rows of white-tipped cylinders
beseeching from brilliantly colored boxes—
Rothmans, Goldflake, Players, Majors—
coffin nails that augured devil-may-care adulthood—
abstractions much to be desired by foolish girls
raised on religion, romance and rock 'n roll.

Shopfronts and telephone poles sped by like skittles
plastered with posters, their words flying
like runaway rooks flapping black feathers
in the air. A diet of letters whose radio jingles
jangled with the bus-stop bell, the harbor foghorn
and the churches' chimes summoning us
to mumbled Latin, an alphabet soup
of suggestive almost-meaning, elusive allusion,
the starvation diet of my dreams.

This

Beneath its thick hide the pale
green inside of this avocado
is tender to the touch.

When I press its flesh,
it presses back again
like youthful skin.

I sit by the glass door
gazing out at the yard
where everything—

bird feeder, solar lantern,
stone statue in the garden—
wears a dunce's cap of snow.

Duns Scotus, the thirteenth century
Scottish philosopher for whom
the word was coined, himself coined

the concept of haecceity or "thisness,"
the quality of a thing that makes it
unique, describable as "this (one)."

I can discern no visible difference between
the finches on the feeder, each one dressed
in the same lackluster winter plumage.

But things look different to avian eyes.
Blind as a kitten in their ultraviolet world
of gleam, shimmer and glint,

I cannot tell "this bird" from "that."
I am glad to say this avocado I have spread
on a piece of rye toast, adding

a pinch of sea salt that brings
the taste of ocean to my lips,
along with an image of that vast

blue-green flatness a child
might imagine as the end of the world,
is behaving just as expected.

Syntax

Outside the Whole Foods Market
a woman with a fistful of fliers
is collaring customers to tell them
the weather forecast—

one hundred degrees this weekend
the hottest since 1931! as though
announcing The End of Days
and perhaps she is.

Over the clanging grocery carts
and the sullen hum of the freezer
a song is playing—
There's a hole in my heart
that can only be filled by you.

How visceral. Ever since I had to cook
Stuffed Sheep's Heart in Domestic Science
class at school, I haven't been able
to view the heart as anything
other than a meaty red muscle.

There's a hole in the ozone too
and I think about that
as I emerge shivering
from the arctic air-conditioning.

But fair play to the blood red Cardinal
in the tree above my head
who has just now added
a three-twanged coda
to the cadence of his prayer
in praise of the ball of hot plasma
otherwise known as the sun.

Any Questions?

When a waiter or waitress suddenly
materializes beside my table
in the dim corner of a downtown café
and asks, "Do you have any questions?"
and "Have you been helped?"
I always consider a literal response:

"Yes, I have many questions"
and "No, not nearly enough."

"What is your area of expertise?"
is a question I would also like to ask,
"and what are your qualifications
for meeting my needs?"

Yet how marvelous to think a perfect stranger
might approach me on the street one day
and offer to answer all my questions—
What makes you get up in the morning?
Why do people fall in love with cars?—
I want to weep with gratitude.

Instead, I pick up the menu,
smile, say "Yes" and "No."

The Bird of Praise

Sometimes the bird of praise flies in and perches
on my shoulder, ruffling his iridescent feathers,
preening with a glad eye on the mirror. He turns

the pages of my new poetry collection with his beak,
pausing at the Acknowledgements Page, the bio,
the mug shot. *Sweetsweetsweet, youyouyou,* he sings

tweaking the silver bauble that dangles from my ear.
Then fickle, flighty fool, he's off, zigzagging away
to some younger, more attractive, more timely poet

who writes about topical events with passionate
intensity, skewering her victims with similes,
uplifting the hapless with her figurative stirrings.

The bird of praise never sticks around for long.
He's always flying off to find new talent he can coo over.
I'd like to cage that bird and keep him for myself.

I'd like to trim my hat with his flashy tail feathers.
God knows I need reminders—alright, lies—
that I am and always will be fairest of them all.

A Call to Prayer

My students, gathered around a long wooden table
are staring at their small rectangular phones
occasional smiles playing over their lovely faces

as they communicate with the invisible ones
those absent friends they seem to prefer
to their flesh and blood sisters who sit quietly

inscrutable as nuns in a silent order.
I think of The Poor Clares who chose lives
of austerity and holiness, only permitted

to glimpse the world through small rectangular
grilles and never speak except inwardly
to God and his intermediaries.

These young women lost in adoration
fondle their phones like sacred objects
the way my mother used to clasp her Sunday missal

lips dutifully following the Latin tongue.
She sat, stood, genuflected to heavenly cues
far beyond my earthly earshot.

On silent retreats at the convent school
I too spoke to invisible friends in high places
begging them for favors, making deals

offering false promises to try harder to be good.
I messaged them incessantly but, unlike the friends
of these student acolytes, they never returned my texts.

Springtime at Starbucks

In the midafternoon gloom
a clatter of girls busy
ignoring each other, thumbs
like butterfly wings fluttering
over the faces of their phones.

Nearby a man sits spellbound
by the eerie radiance
of his laptop screen, fingers
flying over the keyboard,
faint faraway smile curling his lip.

Across the street the trees
are glorious as geishas.
They shake out showers of blossoms
like bridesmaids tipsy after
too many champagne toasts.

I am remembering a night in the Bowery
when we turned a corner and there
was lamplight and merengue music
pouring from the open door of a café,
women in red dresses laughing
and dancing on the sidewalk.

The light was golden,
the women's dresses were fire,
the music thick as syrup,
and we were dazzled by
the beauty of the unexpected.

We might have missed that moment
had we listened to our friends
who warned us not to walk at night,
two gullible white women
alone together. Call a cab,
keep your heads down, don't
talk to dark-eyed strangers.

Back at Starbucks the trees
are flirting madly with passersby.
Dance with us, they say,
we're dressed to the nines.
Help us out, we're dying up here.

The Pancake Artist

She only cooked them once a year
on Shrove Tuesday so we didn't dwell
on the looming Lenten fast
as we raced home after school
to see her lift down the big black frying-pan
and heat it over the blue gas burner
until the fat spat and sizzled.

She'd hoist the milk jug full of batter,
pour a creamy stream into the pan,
tilting and tipping it to a seamless circle.
We hovered famished at her elbow
as the humps and craters formed—
brown sienna over khaki, burnt
umber over buttermilk. It was all

in the timing. One flick of her gifted wrist
and she'd landed it like a fish
on your plate. You rolled it with sugar,
a squeeze of lemon, scarfed it down.

Then it was back to the end of the queue
until your turn returned again.
No rest for her aching shoulders
until we were all contented sinners,
licking our lips, as full as eggs.

Polishing the Floor

As though the rules had been laid down
by the implacable god of the Old Testament
who demanded an accounting of stewardship,
they observed a clear division of duties—

his in the outside world of work and wages
or working his magic in our backyard garden,
hers in the kitchen with its endless round
of cooking, cleaning, making do.

But some tasks required his tensile strength
and practical skills—wallpapering, painting,
sharpening the knives—so dull they wouldn't cut butter
she said beforehand and had blades like rapiers after.

On floor polishing day the kitchen table
with its mismatched chairs and other
indiscriminate bits of furniture
were taken out of the living room to reveal
a suddenly vast expanse of red linoleum.

He opened the tin of Mansion floor wax,
ladled thick orange paste in plopping gobs
all over the floor—
smells of beeswax, turpentine,
linseed oil with notes of *Irel* Coffee—
and spread it out with a long-handled swab.

Then it was our job to don several pairs
of his holey socks and skate all over the floor
to make it shine.

We twirled and pirouetted,
excited, laughing, showing off—
look at me—and me—remembering
the one and only time we saw ice skating
when they took us to the ballet on ice
in the National Stadium's converted boxing-ring
and we imagined ourselves gliding
across the polished surface
on freshly-sharpened blades,
wearing skirts that showed off our knickers,
on legs that went all the way to Sligo.

The Window

I never met my grandfather,
a stoker on a steamship
who died at 57 of pneumonia.

But our mother loved him
and she made us feel as if
we had known him too.

Her gift was to put us there
with her in the tiny house
at the top of the cobbled street,

kicking her button boots
against the rungs of a chair,
a ribbon straggling by her ear

as she watched for his burly
shadow at the window,
the outline of his sailor's cap

and the big canvas seabag
slung over his shoulder.
We could almost hear

his deep-voiced Dublin accent,
smell the salt and sweat of him,
the wet aroma of his woolen jumper

after weeks away at sea.
Her sadness when she talked about
my poor father, my poor mother.

It is only now, among these freshwater
lakes and rivers, far from the sea,
I understand exactly what she meant.

The Sinking of the *Isolda*

December 19, 1940

You stand in the rain, drenched, miserable
waiting for the double-decker bus
when suddenly there it is thundering
toward you like a rogue elephant
the way desire came lumbering along
when you least expected it
in the body of a man who looked
nothing like your dreamboat lover
except for the color of his eyes
and the salt taste of his skin
that evoked your mother
her absence still a tangible ache.

The first time you visited his house
stepping out of the daytime glare
into the shutter-shaded living room
you caught the elbow-greased warmth
of orange floor wax mingling
with the smell of the apple pie
he had just finished making
rolling the pastry out on a wooden board
that was stowed away neatly after use.

No wonder you glommed onto him
for dear life, the way Uncle Christy
must have glommed onto the wreckage
when his ship the *Isolda* went down
off the Wexford coast in 1940.

A German bomber, flying in so low
the men could see the red cross
was in fact a swastika, hit her directly
above the six-foot-high words
"Lighthouse Service" and the blue
ensign on her starboard side.
The ship staggered like a drunken sailor
as Christy and the others toppled out
over the side. He had never learned to swim
but clung doggedly to a spar and did not drown.

Came back to regale his relatives
on summer Sunday evenings
over games of *Beggar My Neighbor,*
Gin Rummy, and endless cups of tea.

When you found yourself foundering
in the wilderness of late twentieth century
North America, you cast about
for something solid, dependable.

How his rich voice resonated
thrumming like a lifeboat
over the roar of wood splintering
everything coming apart.

Idle Hands

The other night a friend asked why
I was always cooking and cleaning
while she just sat there chatting,
drinking wine at my kitchen counter.

Why not stop for a while, have a drink, do nothing?

I trailed my hands in the soapy water,
letting this hitherto unthinkable idea
sink in for a moment, picturing
the distant planet of the past
where women were always busy—

Aunt Veronica forever poring over patterns
for pullovers to manufacture
on her magical knitting machine.

Aunt Nancy and her neighbors knitting madly,
never glancing at their needles
as they leaned over the garden hedge
to swap the latest scuttlebutt.

Aunt Kathleen who never married,
doing *nixers,* decorating wedding cakes
with spun-sugar couples for her shopgirl friends.

Granny's needle always flying, sewing clothes
to deck the family out for sepia-toned photos
in their Sunday best.

Even our mother, ever a diffident housekeeper,
was a dab hand at the soda bread, sauces,
puddings and pastry.

They have long since laid down their needles,
pins and wooden spoons. Their hands are still,
Rosary beads twined in their tired fingers.

I gazed down into the soap bubbles as if
I could see them there in living miniature
like tiny figures waving from snowdomes
on a kitchen shelf. What are my labors
but a kind of posthumous devotion?

Of Saints and Secrets

It has been said that when Saint Ambrose
was an infant, sleeping openmouthed in his crib,
a swarm of bees flew into his mouth.

Whether they stung him or flew out again
is not recorded in the annals of the saints.

It was also said he would become an orator
with honeyed tongue. Imagine sermons
sweet as flowers, ambrosia of his golden words
now lost to history's dark hive.

It takes a million flowers to make a pound of honey
so Irish bees have been busy ever since
they followed Sixth century Saint Modomnóc
from Wales to Ireland, clinging to the sails
of his ship as it flew over the waves toward home.

When the Saint became a hermit,
some bees renounced the hubbub of the hive
for the fields and flowers of the countryside.
Their solitary task—to mate and die
unencumbered by the job of parenting
or allegiance to a queen.

No wonder later monks adopted beehive huts
for their saintly ruminations.

There will be no drones in *this* hive,
our mother used to say—an empty threat
from a woman who could not bear to hurt a fly.
But when our aunt came issuing decrees,
we whirred with joy like worker bees
relieved to be assigned our proper roles.

*Apple jelly, my jam tart, tell me
the name of your sweetheart.*

Mother said to tell our secrets to the bees
who knew how to keep it to themselves,
unlike the neighbors who would
live in your ear if you let them.

My Parents Were Always Kneeling

Father praying by the bed
in his pajamas, embarrassed
when I peeked around
the bedroom door and saw him
vulnerable, nearly naked.
Strange to see that stern man
with his shoulders bowed,
humbling himself to God.

Mother always genuflecting
in churches and in chapels like the one
on Convent Road, Dun Laoghaire.

On Sunday afternoons the light
was golden, the little chapel
dark and full of mystery.

Candles flickered, casting shadows
on the plaster faces of the saints
who gazed benevolently down upon
the upturned faces of the supplicants.

Mother absorbed in prayer
and I absorbed in watching her,
wondering even then at her
unwavering belief which I
steadfastly refused to emulate.

In Ísle Brí (in low spirits, Irish)

"My love she's like some raven at my window with a broken wing"
—Bob Dylan, "Love Minus Zero/No Limit"

This morning a miasma of despair
and disconnection although
the birds are working their usual
dawn chorus of trills and twitterings,
rusty Bluejay screeches
overlying the swanky twang
of the Cardinal's mouthharp.

Seems it has always been this way,
the disease that was in remission
broken out again like measles.

These days an epidemic of gratitude
poems enumerating small wonders
close at hand—a rose,
a red-bellied woodpecker—
to distract us from news of war,
wildfires and weapons sales,
blind faith and faithless politicians.

I consult the Cornell Ornithology app
to learn that a birder might call me
one of the lesser-spotted poets,
author of a handful of books,
recipient of a few small awards.

A shy flycatcher, jealous of
the gaudy plumage, the avian
relationships of other species,
always the migrant genetically
predisposed for departure.

A bird never flew on one wing,
my mother used to say
when I pecked at my food.
And an empty sack won't stand,
my father would echo
with one of his rural metaphors.

I read about the Northern Shrike
who sings to attract other birds as prey,
then impales them on a rough thorn
or barbed wire fence for safekeeping

the way my father hung his shot
pheasants on the kitchen door
to age and tenderize.

They were so beautiful, those
dead things in their funereal finery.
No wonder I could not bear to eat them.

Signs of Bad Weather

After reading an interview with my grandfather, Bill Goggins, of Tullaghanoge, County Meath, Ireland, conducted by his twelve-year-old daughter Ann for a national oral history project in 1938.

When the sky is red in the morning
When the sky is yellow at sunset
When the sun sets down in a bed of clouds
When the sun is greenish
When the seabirds come inland
When the hills are near
When the cows lie down in the field
When swallows fly low
When the crickets cry loudly
When the frogs turn black
When the midges are wicked in the evening
When the dog eats grass
When curlews cry
When the cats turn their backs to the fire

Then it is time to turn inward and ask ourselves
the questions we have placed on the long finger—
Why is a furrow like a backbone?
Why does the warm air seem kind?
Why does lavender keep moths away?
What would it be like to be invisible, like an angel?
What is given and what must be earned?

Tissue Paper

Father kept his rolls of colored tissue
in the cupboard under the stairs
to wrap the gorgeous flowers he grew—
blue irises, prickly pink roses,
dense chrysanthemums, huge
moonfaced dahlias full of earwigs—

so he had to give the whole thing
a shake before placing it just so
on the crinkling sheets, the elegant flowers
like dancers in toe shoes and tutus
peeking out from behind a tear
in the theater curtain.

With a quick flick of his wrist
he created graceful cones
to be conferred on smiling aunts
and on the churlish nuns at school.

The aunts praised father's gallantry,
sometimes glancing askance at their husbands
who liked to back a horse or have a drink
instead of working themselves
into a muck sweat in their
rented backyard gardens.

The nuns accepted flowers on god's behalf
but could not love them openly.
Never buried their noses in the bouquets
to inhale their heavenly scent, but only
placed them on high altars out of reach
for some cold effigy to savor.

I wondered at the waste of all that toil
and artistry, that beauty that would wither in a week.
But was not old enough to question why
god needed cut flowers in the first place,
or a harem of virgins dressed in black
to sing his praises morning, noon and night.

Sweet Aftons

On Saturdays my father used to savor
all his small indulgences—a packet
of ten *Sweet Aftons* and *The Meath Chronicle,*
the ink still wet on its whispery pages.

He would sit in his armchair by the fire,
a fragrant cigarette between his fingers,
the newspaper open on his lap,
reading the news of friends and relations,
who had won the All-Ireland Hurling match,
who had married, who had died.

The half-closed packet lay on the table,
its gold calligraphy curling over the side:
Flow gently, sweet Afton! amang thy green braes,
Flow gently, I'll sing thee a song in thy praise.

It was a message from another continent
like Robert Louis Stevenson's drooping mustache,
Nathaniel Hawthorne's high starched collar
or Louisa May Alcott's elaborate ringlets
on the pack of *Authors* playing cards
that Mammy's cousin sent over from America.

Or the forlorn lovers separated by a cruel father
who gazed at each other from the blue-and-white
world of her willow-pattern plates—
a promise of poetry, of mystery, of everything
I dreamed about but couldn't name.

At Christmas we saved the empty packets
to dress in wrapping paper, tie up with ribbons,
dangle enticingly from the tree. Beautiful
we thought them, who knew nothing of art.

Shine

How I loved to watch my father
polishing our shoes on Sunday mornings
as the first bell rang for Mass.
White shirt sleeves rolled to the elbow,
muscles pumping as he wielded brushes,
a final flourish with the shammy cloth,
then our glowing brogues lined up
in a row on the red linoleum
like little soldiers of Christ.

If only he had not berated our mother
for the state of our clothes, fumed
while she was putting on her lipstick,
shamed her by racing up the street
to Our Lady of Victories ahead
of her hurrying steps, he might have
earned a more Christlike comparison.

Isn't he a terrible man, she would ask
rhetorically as she struggled to tie
the flimsy chiffon scarf beneath her chin.
*Rushing on ahead like the clappers
as if he was ashamed to be seen with us.*
As if we children cared with our four
pairs of feet encased in their shiny shoes
already pointed away from the past.

Yet even now in foreign cities,
lacking one iota of religious belief,
I visit churches to light white votive candles,
pay homage to their long hard labor
and remember their romantic souls,
their spit-shone servitude.

The Joyful Mysteries

Like the list of side-effects recited
sotto voce in television ads
for pharmaceutical solutions,

the glorious characteristics
of the Blessed Virgin—
Tower of Ivory, House of Gold, Ark of the Covenant

followed by the chorus
of monotonous responses
Pray for us, pray for us, pray for us

that arose from the corners of the room
where we knelt in front of wooden chairs
to say the Family Rosary.

Mysterious words like portents
from a parallel universe. Like the fireplace
in our living room, identical twin

to the one in the adjoining sitting room,
separated by a wall but sharing
a single chimney.

Or the Colonial saltbox house whose massive
central chimney with seven flues met
on the second floor to form a huge beehive shape.

A short step to the notion of three persons
in one god. The Unknown then vast
as the Sea of Galilee where Jesus

walked on the water without
getting his feet wet although no one I knew
had ever seen him do it.

Speaking of Things That Are No Longer in Use

my brother had a globe of the world that rested
on a swiveled stand so you could spin it
around to any country you chose.

It was mostly blue for the oceans
and faded pink for what was left
of the unspeakable British Empire.

Our country was a small green speck
hanging off the edge of Europe.
How could that be where we lived?

If you inserted a fingernail carefully into the seam
just above the Equator, the globe split into two
empty halves like an artificial Easter egg.

Then all sorts of things could be hidden inside.
When you walked by and saw it sitting innocently
on its axis, you would know its secrets.

I once hid a box of chocolates there
and could hardly contain myself until Mother's birthday.
She liked the chocolates but didn't seem impressed

with my ingenuity. It was always the way
with my grandiose ideas, exposed
as foolish in the bright light of day.

Mother's own head was like a globe
full of characters and conversations
with God, the angels and the patron saints.

She could map the topography of her inner world
from Heaven at the northernmost point
to the entrance to Hell at the southern tip.

In between lay Purgatory, only a temporary
hell, and the holy souls who needed
our prayers to get out of jail.

We knew our ovoid-shaped souls floated somewhere
in our chests, smooth as polished rocks but lighter,
unattached to muscle, bone or ligament,

while the sharp slopes and dangerous declivities
of our physical bodies went unmapped
and also unexplored, as far as we knew.

Making Strange

> Instructions on a packet of *Strepcils*: "Consult your doctor if symptoms persist or anything unusual happens."

There's nothing strange with us,
my brother says on the phone from Ireland.
Is there anything strange with you?

No, nothing strange with us, I tell him,
except the image of your face on FaceTime
and the miracle of our transatlantic conversation.

He's only making strange, the young mother
apologizes, gently removing the screaming infant
from a stranger's arms.

Strange how we cling to our initial narratives,
half-truths we tell about ourselves,
our flaws and failings, ignoring

everything we have accomplished
since leaving home. I like the strange taste
of certain sounds, as in the colors

ultramarine, cochineal, crimson.
In names like *Imogen* and *Archibald*.
In words like *clavicle, iris, serpentine.*

There's nothing strange, I say
into the magic mirror of my mobile phone,
absolutely nothing and everything.

Black Babies

Ireland 1959

We bought them on the black market
at cut-rate prices from
the Daughters of the Heart of Mary,
those patron saints of fundraising.

They handed out the pictures,
each with a curlyheaded baby face
encircled by a pale halo of dots.

For every penny brought to school
you could prick one of the dots
with a pin. Then when the halo
was complete, came the honor
of picking a baptismal name.

I imagined Deepest Darkest Africa
overrun with little Angelas, Marys,
Eileens, maybe even a Michael or two.

Some of us felt cheated when we learned
the babies would have to stay at home.
We would never get to see them,
never get to fondle their angelic curls.

But we had given them a life of sorts
through the sacrament of Baptism,
our pennies posted to the Foreign Missions
where nuns risked life and limb

(we had seen the pictures of the lepers'
missing noses, missing feet,
in black and white on jumpy screens
in the Assembly Hall),

to bring those little sinners home
into a fold that was full of the whitest
sheep we could imagine.

Cures for Insomnia

Mother used to recommend
a decade of the Rosary
but nowadays when I wake
in the quiet darkness of 3 a.m.,
my long-lost clothes
come back to haunt me
in their multicolored hues
of recrimination and regret.

I imagine them hanging
on hooks like sides of beef
or huddled like a flock of sheep
while I, the sleepless shepherd,
count them one by one.

There are the flounced skirts,
pinafores and smocks,
blue jeans bell-bottomed
with corduroy triangles,
Nehru jackets, Indian blouses
stitched with mirrors,
the poncho made
from a woolen blanket
with a hole in the middle
for my head to appear
like a brown-headed cowbird
fostered in a thrush's nest.

Other clothes materialize
as if to punish me
for their abandonment:

How could you, says
the raspberry wool scarf
lost on a train in Germany.

And what about me, asks
the blue-and-white vintage dress,
with my glad neck
and the tiny pearl buttons
down my bodice?

On Saturday mornings in Dublin
I would scour the ancient markets
where black-clad women
behind wooden stalls called out
  "a pair of trousers for your husband
  or a man's suit for two-and-six."

For half of nothing I acquired
a 1940s gown in which
I swanned around the city,
dragging the dead weight
of Frye boots for ballast.

Are versions of my younger selves
still living somewhere in those
discarded garments that I sewed
so ineptly they never matched
the ones I had imagined,
like a poem that never measures up
to the poem in your head?

Swinging Boats

Sometimes it seems as if your life
is all about trying to balance
on a swinging boat, the painted kind
you used to love at the old time
carnival on Dun Laoghaire Pier.

It wasn't Coney Island but what
did you know of foreign parts?

The helter-skelter where you slid
hell-for-leather on a burlap mat
down a winding metal chute
seemed to go on for miles
what with all the howling kids
and the general hullabaloo.

The swinging boat was gaudily daubed
in blue and yellow swirls, slung
like a cradle between two spars.
A man in a lead-colored coat
and tweed cap took your money.

Then you stepped in one end
your sister in the other
and you pulled on the ropes in tandem
to make the boat sway back and forth
like a clockless pendulum.

It wasn't Venice but what
did you know of gondoliers?

Some days, caught up
in the endless round of tasks
dictated by your *To Do* list
as if your frantic busyness
were a requirement for sainthood
or a penance for past iniquities
you might be a carousel pony
galloping in everlasting orbit
or a girl clad in a secondhand frock
going nowhere fast in a swinging boat.

A Fine Romance

Typewriters are so romantic, my student says,
especially for writing poetry. I pause,
remembering the clattering chorus—
the-quick-brown-fox-jumped-over-the-lazy-dog—
the discordant orchestra of distant secretarial school.

If only I had known that Dickens, Shaw
and my other literary loves had written
in Pitman shorthand, I might have mastered
the secret code invented by a man, practiced—
or so I thought—only by women.

If only I had known the manual typewriter
as the mouthpiece of poetry, not symbol
of my servitude. That somewhere
in small rooms above the shop or stable
there were women poets facing Royals,
Smith-Coronas, Underwoods, tapping out
their thoughts into words made flesh
that dwelt amongst us. Instead the string

of dismal secretarial jobs at which I typed up
scads of scrawling words, stitching a garment
I could never hope to wear, for those
with better things to do than turn a knob
to feed a sheet of paper round a cylinder,
depress the shift key to create a capital,
lift the line-space lever to adjust the margins.

If only I could disconnect the machine
from the Madam, stern-faced supervisor
of the typing pool, forget the little bottles
of liquid eraser to paint over my mistakes,
the infernal clang of the carriage returning home.

In the Adirondacks There Is a Town Called Paradox

When you were finally admitted
to the adult library
with its sepulchral silences,
its dark wood walls,
shelves of hardbacked books,
signs that read "Quiet Please!"
and the frowning librarian
seated behind glass,
you pulled a book of photographs
down from on high,
laid it on a polished table
and drew up a chair.

The book fell open
to a black-and-white image
of emaciated men, a row
of living skeletons propped
against each other outside
a Polish concentration camp.

And you could not stop looking,
could not stop sneaking back each Saturday
to stare as though titillated by terror,
the pure pornography of pain.

How could this be the world
in which your parents lived?

Everywhere crucifixes,
crowns of thorns, bleeding hearts,
saints shot with arrows.

But this was different, real.

How to hold those horrors
with the other images in your head—
that child at the beach
holding her sister's hand,
both of them running
to and from the waves,
squealing with delight.

Your little garden lush
with tulips whose delicate petals
almost immediately begin
their leisurely fall
like a woman in slow motion
shrugging off her blouse,
letting it drop to the ground
in a pile of rumpled yellow silk.

Clematis clad in dark maroon,
replaced by roses
spiky as sea urchins.

Barely time to grieve
the purple iris with its yellow eye
before pink peonies appear,
bowing their heavy heads
like guilty children.

Maybe genuflecting
is all that you can do.

Past Life Regression Moryah

> The Irish phrase *mar dhea* /"mor ya" is characteristic of Irish English speech. A skeptical interjection used to cast doubt, dissent or derision (or all three) on whatever phrase or clause precedes it.

In a previous life I would have been a scullery maid
and you the stable boy, all grimy with horse-sweat
and saddle-soap, wearing the dreamy look of the artist
you'd become after several unexpected incarnations.

We'd meet in the kitchen sometimes. You with a basket
under your arm, me lugging a load of laundry.
I'd admire your fine grey eyes, note your broad shoulders
under the workman's leather waistcoat.

Because you had no sisters you'd befriend me,
sympathize with my shabby treatment
at the rough hands of the Under Housemaid.
When I'd whimper that I hated dusting,

couldn't master *blancmange* for love nor money,
you'd dry my tears with the tail of your cambric shirt,
say I wasn't cut out to be a servant,
that I should have been a poet instead.

That one remark would dribble into my ear
like rain on a parched summer garden.
I'd keep it hidden next to my mother's ring
and the holy picture of my patron saint

under my pillow in the attic. Imagine it
breeding in the cellar of my soul like a dark tuber,
tendrils reaching out to neighbors in the compost heap,
twining over the woodpile, sleuthering up to the rose bush.

And there it would have to incubate, waiting
for the twentieth century to complete its work
of post-Colonial amnesia. Or perhaps deliverance
would come sooner when you'd wait for me
one evening in the kitchen garden, among
the fragrant Stock and Cushion Spurge
whose Latin name—*Euphorbia Polychroma*—
delighted my tongue when you described

its electric yellow bracts blooming on low cushions
in late April. It was then I knew I'd run straight out
the back door and into your arms, abandoning
the washing and the mistress's querulous complaints,

into whatever future might be waiting,
closing the wrought-iron gate behind me.

Out in Left Field at Dodgertown, Florida

A smattering of fans in the bleachers.
Behind them dark palm trees poised
against a leaden sky like a water-balloon
about to burst.

Groups of tanned enthusiasts
sporting neon-colored teeshirts
shorts and visored hats arrive
and settle into their seats.

When the skies suddenly open
we run to pack ourselves neat
as a crate of Indian River oranges
into a shelter overlooking homeplate
on the washed-out baseball diamond.

Aromas of onions, mustard, pickles
mingle with lush smells of the tropics—
a Dodger-blue bowl of citrus fruit
gone soft in the heat.

It might be Ellis Island and I
a displaced immigrant hiding behind
my notebook's paper wall for all
that I can fathom this melodrama

in which everyone seems to know
what to wear, what to eat, what to say on cue
like the songs in a musical I've never seen
but all of the others know by heart.

Last Time I Saw My Sisters

one was peering at a recipe
for risotto, the other
at the microscopic script
in an obsolete telephone book.

We traded magnifiers for
our failing eyesight, faded
like the bygone brown
of our collectively colored hair.

We were like the *Greae*
old from birth, who lived
in the white foam
on the waves of the sea
and rejoiced to share
one eye among them.

Things I Never Say Aloud

My sister who lives
halfway across the world
wants to meet in Dublin
when the pandemic is over.

We'll stay in a fancy hotel,
walk on the beach we loved
as children where we picked up
smooth flat stones to take home
for endless games of Shellybeds.

We'll go walking arm-in-arm,
window-shop and revisit old haunts,
eat *Tayto* crisps and Cadbury's chocolate.
We'll gossip and remember.

I think of my aunt turning away
from my mother's hospital bed in tears.
Her only sister and best friend,
keeper of shared secrets
we could not yet imagine.

Say an aspiration for her,
she whispered and I felt
the familiar flare of anti-Catholic anger—
my only safeguard against grief.

Now, when I think of planting bulbs
and the spring garden
that will emerge after winter,
I keep wanting to add
the old people's caution—
if we're spared.

Motherhood

> "Many young mothers suffer from post-mortem depression."
> —Excerpt from a student essay

And you thought death
would be the end of it.
But there is no end
to motherhood and all
its attendant trespasses.

A state you arrive at like
a novice entering the convent,
all pure intention,
prayerfulness.

At twenty, you never think
about bequeathing sadness
misery, despair.

It's all about perfect teeth,
clear eyes, intelligence.
Adelle Davis and her Nazi
nutritional schemes
for breeding the Super Race.

For a long time, years perhaps,
you are the breast, perfect
center of the universe,
the home planet.

Then things change. One Sunday
the father dusts off his baseball glove
and it's all over for you,
girl who can't catch a ball
to save your life.

Feeding the Wild Rabbit

"We carry our homes within us which enables us to fly."
—John Cage

What should I feed the wild rabbit
that has been leaving its scat
in the snow under the birdfeeder?
I saw it sitting still as a garden statue
when I arrived home yesterday at dusk.

Last week the rechargeable bulb
of the amaryllis, banished to a shelf
in the back of the garage,
sprang to life and threw out first
one green shoot and then another.

Do animals dream of the coming light
in their lairs beneath the snow?
I dream constantly of homelessness.
Something is preventing me
from entering those places I once lived,
all doors locked against me.

Once there was a room whose only light
came from a glowing fire where all
the crisscrossed bones of my ancestors
burned like kindling and their strange
elongated shadows leaped the walls.

For two nights now I have dreamed
of skating barefoot on a river
covered with a skiff of snow.

On either side the trees and bushes
look like lavish wedding gowns
adorned with lace. My feet glide
effortlessly over the ice. No fear
of falling, no searching for
safe harbor. Just this flying.

Inchigeelagh Getaway

Gaeilge, Inse Geimhleach, meaning "Island of the Hostages"

The land is a sponge sodden
with salt water and rain,
the mossed path a tangle
of Herb Robert and buttercup.
Giant leaves of gunnera
and the green spears of rushes
stand guard around the pond.
Laburnum hangs its head
like a girl drying her yellow hair.

Water gushes under culverts
over rocks, tap-tapping on the roof
of the sunroom like a timid visitor.

Through rain-streaked windows
I can see our hosts raise their heads
to look upward as the tempo
intensifies to an irascible hammering;
almost hear the ebb and flow
of their soft voices
from where I stand hidden
under a canopy of dripping roses
and dangling fuchsia blossoms.

A clattering sound as three
runaway sheep hoof it down the lane
like boys going over the wall
to mitch from school.
Tomorrow they will have to return,
tails between their legs.

But for now they are part
of a thrilling spectacle as they trundle
three abreast into the green gap
between the high ditches.

The other sheep graze the wet grass,
their plaintive bawling
from the nearby field
like the call-and-response
of a gospel choir
singing the praises of
another doomed rebellion.

The Suspension of Disbelief

New England Circus Day 100 years ago—
mills and factories stood abandoned
as people flocked to see the tricksters,

freaks and misfits who rolled in
on colored wagons, dragging cages
full of sullen, maybe stolen, animals.

Elephants with shackles around
their tree-trunk legs, lions and tigers
roaring, rattling their restraints.

Ringmasters ready to swindle
a populace desperate for a little
innocent debauchery.

Crowds gathered for the Russian
Acrobats who flew above them
like graceful birds.

A boy peering through a hole
in the bottom of the Big Top
might have noted that their tattered tutus,

shabby tights, their raddled greasepaint
was a little tawdry, only a gaudy counterfeit
that shamed him for his prying eyes,

his eagerness to believe in omens,
auguries, his fascination with the far-off,
the unfamiliar, and the foreign.

Blood Moon

Neighbors appear in ones and twos
to cluster outside the buildings.
Some have brought folding chairs,
others binoculars, as though expecting
fireworks and not a lunar eclipse.

Those with the best equipment
relay the news to the rest of us.
But everyone can see a shadow begin
to move across that unearthly countenance—
a woman covering her hair
with a black lace mantilla
as she hastens shamefaced
through the side door of a church.

Now the moon is a blood orange
in a bowl of stars. Some burst
into applause and others follow.

Our moon, they murmur proudly,
proprietary as children watching Mother
get tarted up for a night on the town,
awed by her transformation from
domestic drab to celestial queen—
the old familiar become untouchable.

Green Up Day at the Superfund Site

Someone found a black magic 8-ball
among the hypodermic needles,
plastic plates, Styrofoam containers.
A robin's nest with a hole in the bottom,
bobbing on a sea of soda bottles,
scrap metal and crushed beer cans.

We picked and picked,
filling our bright green trash bags
with remnants of old blankets,
a soiled puptent, twisted spatula,
burned-out frying-pan,
rusted can-opener, paring knife,
while the seagulls circled overhead
screaming accusations in
their own indigenous languages.

Who were the successive waves
of homeless people that camped
on this poisoned land, then left,
shrugging off everything
they could not carry?

When someone found a tattered copy
Of *The Giving Tree* there were calls
for the creation of an altar to
incongruous artifacts—and we did that.

Domestic Science

April in the country meant
nests were everywhere.
A robin's nest on top
of the back door porch light
made us tiptoe in and out
trying not to disturb the nursery.

A cluster of hexagonal cells
under the eaves signaled
the onset of a wasp's nest
that we sprayed guiltily
with cans of toxic foam
under cover of night.

Hornets chewed wood pulp
mixed with saliva to make
a paper cone, its telltale teardrop
hanging from deck rail like
a malevolent horn of plenty.

Mole-roads ran through soil
like the coiled castings of worms
emerging from the sand at low tide.

We had to halt construction
on a new garage because a Phoebe
made her nest on the light fixture
in the half-constructed ceiling.
Our carpenter downed tools,
refused to continue until
all the chicks were fledged.

A mouse chose the hollow under the carburetor
of the Chevy truck we used for snowplowing
to make a home from scraps of insulation
torn from the inside of the hood.

With every storm its nest was spoiled,
yet it kept returning to the warm engine
like a refugee who comes back to his village
after the shelling has stopped
thinking *maybe this time . . .*

Birds with their beaks full of twigs,
chipmunks' cheeks stuffed with seeds,
spider traps in every crevice.

All that industrious home making,
everyone to-ing and fro-ing
as it was and ever shall be,
world without end.

Soundscape of My Ear

"It's never too late to become indigenous"
—Robin Wall Kimmerer, from *Braiding Sweetgrass*

The last of winter lingers in a small round nest
high in a bare tree, slung like a boat
between two branches.

Mourning dove on the roof
repeating its series of low notes.
Calls and whistles everywhere
despite the dull rumble
of a stumpgrinder at work.

First sign of life in ordered whorls
of sedum, stirring of marsh marigolds,

hyacinths in a pot to bring back
your father's hardworking hands.

Clematis already showing green
will bloom deep red for your birthday.

And just yesterday three brilliant goldfinches
twittering in a tree, forsythia returning
in a yellow Confirmation dress.

That Spring day last year, a meadow by the lake
all flowers and butterflies and birds,
the rise and fall of wings and you alone
and able to take it in for once.

There is no repairing certain sadnesses,
that series of disasters in the past.
Everything is driven forward.
There is no saying no.

Lingering Over It

Today all sweetness and close-up detail—
the bee abuzz on the last of the roses,
a Monarch fluttering on the milkweed.

Hope in the bright belated flower buds
dangling from scarlet spires
of the pineapple sage

although they bloomed too late to be of use
to hummingbirds, long since shimmered off
to warmer time zones.

The whirling butterfly bush refuses
to die back, intent on splaying
its delicate white flowers

out over the spent coral bells,
the ruined spring-blooming clematis.
Behind the trunk of a bare birch tree

a calico cat crouches still as a mummer,
staring into the undergrowth.
Surprise largesse of sun

on into November causes geese
to muster in gaggles on the lake,
honking their confusion—

Isn't it supposed to be winter?
How to find our cue to flee the coming cold
in all this blinkered kindness?

Persistence Hunting

> *"Persistence hunting* is a technique in which hunters use a combination of running, walking, and tracking to pursue prey to the point of exhaustion."
> —BBC documentary

A slag-heap of dirty snow
in front of the *Price Chopper* supermarket.

Salt-stains on our boots.
The cars are filthy.

Robins dip and flit among the branches
devouring dried remains of last year's rosehips.

We raise tired eyes to watch dark shapes
of down-clad pleasure-seekers

hurtling down the distant slopes
like Breughel's dwarvish hunters

returning over the hillside, troubled
almost empty-handed, to their homes.

While below them on the frozen lake
the unconcerned disport themselves

with winter games in what presaged
The Little Ice Age, circa 1565.

Umwelt

Three green parrots, then two more
flying over the rooftops in Rincón.

Hundreds of yellow mangoes fallen
on the ground behind the wire fence

of the pink-painted house across the road,
all their sweet flesh rotting in the heat.

Out on the ocean, pelicans dive-bomb
their prey, gulp it down, then settle back

on the water like bad-tempered old men
grousing about the menu.

Below, a multicolored world of twist and ripple,
flick and riffle of fish grazing the reef's edge,

our faces behind masks and snorkels
bent over them like angels.

Geese—A Love Poem

On the highway's gravel shoulder
a goose with a gaggle of goslings
waddling beside her.

Urban birds so common
they have become forgotten
except for their indiscriminate
droppings on greenways
and golf courses, a menace
to the built environment.

But this noisy brood is perilously
out of place, close to the line
of buses, cars and trucks
that thunder past, a crush
of armor-plated rhinos
kicking up the dust
en route to the watering hole.

You've been watching
all week on television
the frightened faces of refugees
fleeing an invading army,
babies clutched to their chests,
dusty indigo robes flapping,
everything they could salvage
strapped to their backs,
ruined villages smoking
already in the past.

Back on the highway
the goslings' furry heads
move up and down
like bobbleheaded dolls
while the mother tries
to shield them with her body
as if she could withstand
a metal hurricane
with only her feathers
and her warning honks.

Wellfleet

> "Fiddler crabs are so named because the male holds one claw,
> always much larger than the other, somewhat like a violin."
> —Encyclopedia Britannica

In the distance a house on stilts
all its balconies facing the water.

I imagine living there, encircled
by the sea's perpetual music.

Long grass of salt marshes, tidal flats
shallow pools thrumming.

Fiddler crabs appear and disappear
diving and surfacing in an endless rhythm

roiling the sand as they sift and scavenge
for nourishment, pausing only when

the males brandish their colossal claws
to wave at their prospective mates

moving their instruments in unison
like the string section of a surreal orchestra.

Mono Lake, California

A small grey lizard darts away
perfectly dressed to disappear
into the rocky surface. Osprey nests
loll on top of ragged tufa towers.
Alkali flies form a cloud on the water
scatter when we wade among them.

In late summer the flies carpet
the shoreline and California gulls
run along the edges of the lake
beaks open to gather in the glut
like greedy children at a tea party.

No fish can live in this salty stew
which reminds me of the fish we ate
on meatless Fridays of my childhood
when everybody spoke in code:

Put down that yoke and hand me that gazebo.
Would you ever go out and get me the messages?
You'd do it while a cat would be chewing a marble.

And so I thought outlandish places
such as Jericho and Timbuktu existed
only in the stories of Scheherazade
and The Dead Sea was nowhere
on a map but only in my dream
of floating supine in its brine embrace
suspended by the miracle of salt.

The Weight of the World

September, and the world is in its yellow period.
Giant sunflowers bend over us
like benign ogres.

A riot of rough oxeye and goldenrod
in the fields. Final conflagration
before the cold creeps in.

Goldfinches have found the purple spikes
of anise hyssop, now gone to seed.
The plant shakes with their feather weight.

"Angela," the spam text on my phone pings.
"Lose forty-five pounds in two weeks!"
By dint of a little mental arithmetic,

I realize that is more than one-third
of my entire body weight. I think I'll emulate
the woodchuck gorging in the garden,

doing his job of tripling his weight for winter.
He does not appear to question either
his destiny or his diet.

I'll do my best to ignore reductive invitations,
get back to the work of making more
and not less of myself.

On the La Platte

Turtles, motionless as Zen masters,
pose on every sunlit log, practicing
the art of synchronized sitting.

A Caspian Tern, hunched in mid-air,
hovers for a moment before becoming
a missile aimed inexorably at its target.

The Great Blue Heron stands like a stone
in the shallows, teaching us the gift
of patience and of knowing when to strike.

The river, slow and unassuming, holds us
all aloft, the fish and feathered ones,
this human, breathless in her handmade boat.

This Is the Life

I never meant to have—
anise hyssop alive with bees
outside the glass door of the deck.
Emerald hummingbird sucking nectar
through the slender straw of her beak.

You reading aloud to me last night
as I was washing dishes, making dinner,
cleaning out the refrigerator.
Like playing house under the table
with the chairs turned upside-down.

This is the life of the white dog,
spared from work by the color
of its coat, who can sleep
by the fire all day, dreaming
of mountains, counting sheep.

Why I Would Like to Be a River

Because it begins as a whisper
in a lonely place high up
among the bracken and the sedges,
unnoticed, trivial.

At first slender as a girl
collecting sallies in her apron,
a river swells with rainfall,
shrinks with drought,
may slacken to a stingy trickle
or strengthen to a torrent.

Reed buntings skim its surface.
An emerald dragonfly and kingfisher
flit and dazzle above its banks.

Its voice is never jabber, only song.

A river may appear impressionable,
foolish, easily led. And yet,
if turned aside, will in the end
come round to its intended course.

It cannot be contained by fences,
ditches, levees, dams. Leaves
everything it has ever owned
behind it in the past.

It runs its own way home, holding
a kiss in its watery mouth.

About the Author

Angela Patten's publications include four poetry collections and a prose memoir, *High Tea at a Low Table: Stories From An Irish Childhood* (Wind Ridge Books, 2013).

Winner of the 2022 Anthony Cronin International Short Poem Award and other awards, Patten has received artist grants from the University of Vermont, the Vermont Arts Council, and the Vermont Community Foundation. Her work has appeared in many literary journals and in anthologies, including *The Field Day Anthology of Irish Writing* and *The White Page/An Bhileog Bhan: Twentieth-Century Irish Women Poets*.

Born and raised in Dublin, she maintains dual citizenship in Ireland and the U.S. She lives with her husband, poet Daniel Lusk, in Burlington, Vermont, where she is a Senior Lecturer Emerita in the English Department at the University of Vermont.

www.ingramcontent.com/pod-product-compliance
Lightning Source LLC
Chambersburg PA
CBHW031202160426
43193CB00008B/469